It'$ My Money

A Guided Journal to Help You Manage Your Finances

Volume 1

PATRINA DIXON

Cover Design by Alonzo Little of A Little Guidance

ISBN: 1537639463
ISBN-13: 9781537639468

This journal belongs to

_____

ACKNOWLEDGMENTS

I am so grateful for the opportunity to make a dream come true. I am so thankful for the many people who've helped me realize my dream and potential along the way.

I want to thank God who is the head of my life. It is because of Him this is possible.

I also could not have done this without my ever so supportive family: Fred, my loving husband, Kelli, my beautiful daughter, who is also the inspiration behind the title, and Mildred, the best mom in the whole wide world.

I also thank everyone else who's encouraged me throughout this project and offered kind words and honest feedback when I needed it.

TABLE OF CONTENTS

Dear Financial Scholars,

This journal is about you and your money. It is designed to encourage and inspire you to better manage it - at your own pace. Remember it's your money.

As I travel the country speaking to young people, I find a great number of them tend to mismanage their money. Based on admission, most mismanagement is due to lack of income, not budgeting, or lack of understanding the banking system. Most adolescents miss out on the value of saving, investing, and making wise financial decisions until something drastic happens.

The *It's My Money* journal is designed to purposely prepare you for the financial road ahead.

My goal is to help educate and empower individuals to take better care of their money which can ultimately lead to their happiness by increasing in their pride and confidence. Through personal conversations, research, studying, and practical lessons – this journal covers a variety of topics best suited for your development.

The journey of financial success is never ending. Thus, this is only the beginning of a three-part journal series. Soak up the knowledge and begin applying these tips to your daily routines. If you start small, you will be sure to see large gains!

Financially Fit,

Patrina Dixon

It's My Money!

What is financial literacy? Why does it matter?

Imagine someone giving you a check for $50,000 with only one rule: you must invest it. What would you do with your money if you could keep two-thirds of the profit from the investment? Where would you start with developing a financial plan?

Most young professionals are not prepared to deal with the financial challenges of real life as a result of poor preparation, decrease of financial planning in school, and the lack of relevancy until it matters. But why wait until you're in a financial situation to become educated on finances? Why wait until you have the $50,000 check in hand, to create a financial plan for yourself? Why wait until you are a young professional to learn how to manage your finances?

Financial literacy encompasses your ability to understand how money works in the world. It involves earning, saving, spending, and investing money. It is important to be able to apply your knowledge of each in order to set, reach, and surpass your financial goals. Financial literacy is constantly evolving and includes everyday tasks from balancing a checkbook to investing and preparing for retirement. In a world full of options, it would be wise for you to have the knowledge so that you can good decisions as to not live paycheck to paycheck.

So you're probably wondering, *"How do I use this journal? How can it help me with my financial goals?"* This financial journal covers some of the most important financial concepts for you to understand as a teenager and emerging young adult. It includes important vocabulary, short summaries, real life examples, and thought provoking questions to help you better plan for your financial future.

Each chapter begins with an overview. Following each chapter, you'll find a list of essential questions that will help spark conversation, action, and application. Use the pages within the chapter to answer the questions, complete the tasks, and work on the next steps. Allow the quotes to inspire you while you're on your journey to financial success. Everyone's journey is different and unique. Be confident and consistent with your financial goals and document your progress throughout this journal.

Try this simple quiz to see how well you're prepared for the $50,000 check. Be sure to come back to this quiz after you've finished the journal to gauge your understanding and progress.

1. Where would you open your first checking account?
    a. The Federal Reserve Bank
    b. A local bank
    c. A piggy bank
    d. A credit lender

2. What are the reasons you would visit a bank?
    a. Lost your ATM card
    b. Open a bank account
    c. Apply for a loan
    d. All of the above

3. You finally have a summer job. You're making $7 an hour and work a 30-hour week. You get your first check after two weeks of work. Your check is good for:
    a. $7 x 60 hours, or $420
    b. $420 minus taxes
    c. $420 plus a bonus
    d. $420 minus employer expenses

4. Most people who make a lot of money over a long period of time usually:
   a. Do it all by themselves.
   b. Work closely with banks and other financial institutions.
   c. Let other people make money decisions for them.
   d. Do not have to worry about budgets.
   e. Never borrow money.

5. You want to reach a savings goal for something special you've had your eye on. How do you set a savings goal?
   a. Set a dollar amount and deadline.
   b. Save everything you can.
   c. Set aside a specific amount or percentages from your income.
   d. Solicit others to help.

6. You're planning on making a large purchase once you've met your savings goal. How would you spend your money?
   a. Make your purchase without second guessing it.
   b. Compare the purchase at other locations to find the best price.
   c. Wait for the item to go on sale.
   d. Try to talk down the price.

7. You're trying to develop your financial plan. You need to set your goals for your emergency fund. How much should be in your emergency account?
   a. One to three months of expenses
   b. Three to six months of expenses
   c. Six months to a year of expenses
   d. Depend on family and friends to help in an emergency.

8. Credit, what's that? You're familiar with a credit card, but what is a credit score?
    a. An A-F grading scale used to get a credit card.
    b. A three-digit number that is used to describe your credit value history.
    c. An estimate of how much you can borrow from a lender.
    d. The rating on a credit card.

9. If you were in need of financial advice, what would you do?
    a. Keep all of my questions to myself.
    b. Go to social media for advice.
    c. Ask my friends and family what they'd do in my situation.
    d. Seek a professional so I can learn as much as possible and create action steps.

10. Your best friend asks to borrow $1,000 to put his 10th business idea into action. He wants to open a bicycle shop and name it after you. You let him borrow the money only if
    a. You can negotiate the terms of the investment.
    b. He pays you back the money within 30 days.
    c. You ask for partial ownership of the company.
    d. He puts the loan in writing.
    e. All of the above.

BANKING SERVICES

What role can banks and other financial institutions play in helping you manage your money?

Money (bills or coins) is what is used to pay for things that you want, services that you need or to pay people for the work that they do. Money represents the glue that binds people, industry, business opportunities, and financial rewards within our economy. The economy is then fueled by supply and demand, allowing citizens to create, sell, purchase, and profit off goods or services. Where does this leave you? You are both a creator of income and a consumer. You have the option to earn money by working, providing a service or selling a good. As a consumer you have the option to buy specific products or services.

When it comes to banking, how do you know where to start? How do you know what to do with the money you earn? It is wise to open a bank account to monitor your finances. As long as you're under the age of 18, you'll need another adult or co-owner to help you open an account. Typically, this is a trustworthy parent or guardian who can also serve as an advisor. Some parents will create a savings or checking account with spending restrictions in an effort to help manage your funds. In this technology driven world, there is a mobile app and online access for everything – especially when it comes to banking.

You'll be able to login and monitor your account, spending, and savings. You think you can do this alone? Or wonder why do I need a bank account at all? Building a relationship with a bank can be beneficial for you in the long run when it comes to savings, loans, credit, or investment opportunities. Your

11

financial accounts serve as investments into a bank and their programs, thus starting a partnership for more options later. In addition, a professional can advise you on your financial decisions and help you create an action plan to successfully accomplish your goals. Banks pay customers through interest rates to essentially "borrow" their money while managing the account. The amount of the interest varies based on financial institutions and types of accounts. It's best to start off with a simple account as you learn how to manage your own finances.

Next Steps: Discuss opening a bank account with a parent/guardian and a banking specialist.

Essential Questions

Apply the information you've learned

1. What is money, how is it used in our society, and what roles can banks and other financial institutions play in helping you manage it?

2. What are some of the reasons people use banks?

3. What are some examples of how money changes hands in our society? What makes money flow between people, businesses, and banks?

4. What types of bank accounts are there?

5. If you open a checking account, who's responsible for keeping track of how much money is in the account?

6. What might happen if you never compare your records to the bank's records?

7. How will you be sure the bank records for your checking account are correct?

8. How can you access a bank account?

9. What are some of the benefits from having a bank account?

I saw a bank that said 24-Hour banking, but I don't have that much time. —Steven Wright

Friendship is like a bank account; you can't continue to withdraw from it without making a deposit. –Unknown

---

Money looks better in the bank than on your feet.
–Sophia Amoruso

Rebecca's Story

I have a bank account now. At one point, I shared the account with my dad, but now he no longer has access. He only oversees the statements every month to help me with my financial goals.

He's finally starting to trust me – and I'm getting some independence shopping without permission!

I even have my own debit card now – I'm so glad that I can do what I want without checking with my parents for everything. I don't spend much really, I just go shopping with my friends, I might get some food when we go hang out, and I've probably caught a movie or two, but I haven't bought anything major like a computer or anything.

At the end of the month when the bank statement came, my dad had a fit, and said that I spent way too much money! I looked at the statement and didn't realize that a little shopping, eating out, and a couple of movies could add up so quickly!

My dad says I only have one month to get my spending in check, or he'll take my debit card back – I guess I'd better pay more attention to my spending.

Let's Review

1. Do you think that Rebecca needed more information before she got her bank account and debit card?

2. What could she have done differently in order to handle the situation better?

Knowledge is only useful if you apply what you learn. —Benny Esco

---

Saving money isn't about being able to buy bigger and better things. It's about being prepared to take care of your family. −*Dave Ramsey*

Know what you won and know why you own it.
Peter Lynch

_____
_____
_____
_____
_____
_____
_____
_____
_____
_____
_____
_____
_____
_____
_____
_____
_____
_____
_____
_____
_____
_____
_____

CHECKING SERVICE$

"A penny saved, is a penny earned." Benjamin Franklin

As the saying goes, "Money will burn a hole in your pocket!" We always spend cash faster when it sits in our hand, wallet, or pocket – often forgetting how much, where, and when. It's much easier to manage your finances with a checking account. A check is another tool banks provide to help you track the movement of your money.

As a result, you are expected to make frequent withdrawals and deposits into the account. Deposits can be made over the counter at the bank, online, via a mobile app, with a check, or online transfer. You can use checks, make purchases with your debit card, online, or transfer or withdrawals as well. ATM's, or automatic teller machines, offer a chance to make both deposits and withdrawals using your debit card and a four-digit pin specific to your card.

I know you're probably thinking, "Checks are so outdated! Who uses checks nowadays?" Well, everyone. Checks are legal documents that can be used like cash, typically for paying larger expenses. Knowing how to write a check is a necessary fundamental skill to avoid identity theft, debt, fines, or additional fees. When writing a check or using your debit card it may be wise to also balance your checkbook. Balancing your checkbook means making note of how your funds are moving in and out of your account.

Your bank will keep track of this as well, however, it is not as immediate and timely. If you always keep track of your transactions consistently, there will be no surprises when you review your monthly statement.

The next page includes a sample check for you to review. *Pay to the order of* is always the recipient and the dollar amount should be written in words. Your signature will always be the bottom right line. Memo gives you space to write any important details about the purchase for your records.

Next Steps: Decide if a checking account is right for you with an adult and banking specialist. If so, open an account and set goals for your spending and savings plan.

Now, it's your turn to practice completing the checks below for an amount of $65.17 to Wal-Mart for clothes and $77.38 to

Target for house items.

Your name	103
Street Address	
City, State 12345	Date _____
Pay to	
the order of _____	**$** _____
_____	Dollars
Bank	
Street Address	
City, State 12345	
Memo _____	_____

Your name	103
Street Address	
City, State 12345	Date _____
Pay to	
the order of _____	**$** _____
_____	Dollars
Bank	
Street Address	
City, State 12345	
Memo _____	_____

⑈123400056⑈   987654320103

Essential Questions

1. Describe ways, other than cash, that people use to pay for things.

2. Why are checks used? Isn't a check just a piece of paper?

3. What are some reasons that someone might want to pay by check rather than using cash?

4. Suppose someone told you that they could write a check to pay for something even if they knew they didn't have enough money in their checking account to cover the amount of the check. What would you tell this person?

5. What does it mean to write a "bad check?"

6. What are some of the things you can use an ATM to do?

7. What information is needed to write a check?

8. How do you balance a checkbook?

Louis' Story

Hi! I'm Louis Simmons. I got my first bank account at the age of 16. It was a checking account. When we went to the bank, I was handed some temporary checks and told, "Congratulations!" About a week later, my real checks and debit card came in the mail. Both of which did not come with instructions. I had to figure it out all on my own or ask my mom.

I remember going to the bank, trying to fill out a deposit slip in order to cash a check. I quickly realized that I completed the wrong form. I felt so embarrassed. But luckily the bank teller helped me identify the right form and fill it out correctly. The experience helped me appreciate trial and error.

A few weeks later, I wrote a check because I forgot my debit card at home. After practicing at home, I was sure I completed everything correctly. It felt great, except I learned my check bounced. I didn't have enough money in my account and ended up with several fees to pay. This was another lesson for me to learn. I hadn't balanced my checkbook in over a month.

These experiences made me realize that banking isn't something that should be taken lightly – I need to learn how my accounts work, so that I won't make expensive mistakes like I did before – because mistakes like those can end in a financial loss.

Let's Review

1. What are some questions Louis should have asked when he got his materials in the mail?

2. What could Louis have done to be a more successful banker?

Planning is bringing the future into the present so that you can do something about it now.
Alan Lakein

_____
_____
_____
_____
_____
_____
_____
_____
_____
_____
_____
_____
_____
_____
_____
_____
_____
_____
_____
_____
_____
_____
_____
_____
_____
_____

Most people don't plan to fail, they fail to plan.
John L. Beckley

A goal without a plan is just a wish.
Antoine de Saint-Exupery

Wealth consists not having great possessions, but in having few wants. Epictetus

SAVINGS ACCOUNT$

How does a savings account help you accomplish your financial goals? What is the difference between a savings account and a checking account?

Saving is about putting money aside for future use. You can save for personal pleasure, necessities, business related ventures, or an emergency fund. Banks and other financial institutions offer a variety of incentives for people to have savings accounts in addition to a checking. The number one incentive is interest. By simply allowing the bank to protect and borrow your funds in the account, your money can earn interest over time. The amount of interest depends on the type of account, financial institution, and time period. Simple interest is calculated only over a specific amount of time while compound interest is calculated based on the dollar amount in the account and time period.

There is a long list of different types of savings accounts. The most common include regular savings, certificates of deposit (CDs), and money market accounts. Regular savings accounts require a minimum deposit, accrue interest monthly, and usually have limits on deposit and withdrawal amounts. CDs are best for larger balances and often require a larger minimum deposit. In addition, these accounts must be opened for a specific amount of time, known as a term, and often have a penalty if a withdrawal is made prior to the term. Money market accounts allow for limited check writing and withdrawals each month because these accounts usually pay a higher interest over a fixed amount of time.

Just like a checking account, withdrawals, deposits, and transfers can be made using a savings account. When making a deposit or withdrawal at the bank, you'll need to use the appropriate slip. Both forms require personal information, account details, and the amount. Note the differences on the images below.

Next Steps: Decide if a savings account is best for you with an adult and banking specialist. Set personal savings goals. Practice completing the withdrawal and deposit banking slips below.

Essential Questions

1. What is compound interest? How does this help increase your savings?

2. Why is it important to save?

3. Identify at least three to five reasons you need to save.

4. What are some methods in which you can save money or increase your savings?

5. What is your goal for your savings account? How much time will it take you to reach the goal? What is your plan to reach the goal?

6. Describe a moment when you decided to save instead of spend your money.

7. Why would you recommend opening a savings account to someone who doesn't have one yet?

8. Even though the purpose of the account is to save money, why might it be necessary to withdraw money from a savings account? How would you keep track of your transactions?

9. What does "ATM" stand for, and what's the purpose of an ATM? What banking transactions can people do at an ATM?

10. Suppose you put $200 in an account that has simple interest. Once a year the bank will pay you 5% interest on your money. How much interest will you earn in one year?

How many millionaires do you know who have become wealthy by investing in savings accounts? –Robert G. Allen

Save one-third, live off one-third, and give away one-third. –Angelina Jolie

"Pay Yourself First." P. Dixon

An investment in knowledge pays the best interest. Benjamin Franklin

INCOME

How is your cash flow? What can you do to increase your earning power? How will you plan to use your income?

Your earning power is the ability for you to accumulate money in exchange for work. I'm sure by now you've received an allowance just because, chores, or for providing a service for someone else. Some of those services may have included cutting the grass, carrying groceries, selling items, or babysitting. That's a great start, but the real question is how can you maximize your earning potential? Have you thought about using your strengths and skill set to earn money? Take a quick moment and think about three things you enjoy doing that may be profitable. Make a list on the pages that follow.

It's really that easy. The truth is, anything can turn into a profitable service with the right plan. Your plan should include how you can gain income now and what you can do in the future. Some people earn money independently by owning their own ideas, business, or products. Other people earn money by working as an employee for another person or company. Some simple ways to increase your income include 1) increase the time earning income (work more hours), 2) achieve more results in less time, increase the quality of service, and 3) gain new knowledge or additional skills to help you excel.

The key is to have a combination of education and a long list of skills to increase your knowledge, work ethic, value, and marketability. Education breeds discipline, such discipline that

is needed to always evolve by learning new things, skills, and avenues for income. Your level of education and skill set determines the level of income you deserve or should receive with some employers. It's also important to remember that without advanced education or additional skills, a job is only obligated to pay you minimum wage for services or working.

Essential Questions

1. Have you ever earned money for your work? What work did you do and how much did you get paid? Give an example of a time you were paid more for one type of work than for another?

2. Let's say a person wants to earn more money than he does currently. What are some of the things he might try in order to make that happen?

3. If you don't have a job, what are some things you are great at doing that you can provide as a service to others for pay? Write 5.

4. When you think about your own future, what is one type of work or job you have thought about for yourself? Why?

5. What kind of education and skills would you need to succeed in that career? How can you acquire these necessary skills?

6. How can you earn an income from things you already like to do? Write out a plan for what services you can provide, the cost, and how to get clients?

7. Look in the paper or an online sales ad to find an ad for shirts or another product. Create a scenario of how you could go about earning funds to purchase the product.

8. What is meant by the term, "minimum wage"? What is the current minimum wage for workers in your state?

9. Research and compare the education requirements for three different jobs or occupations that interest you.

You cannot be seeking yourself when you're making money. —Felix Dennis

The person who doesn't know where his next dollar is coming from usually doesn't know where his last dollar went. —Unknown

If you work just for money, you'll never make it, but if you love what you're doing and you always put the customer first, success will be yours.

—Ray Krock

_____
_____
_____
_____
_____
_____
_____
_____
_____
_____
_____
_____
_____
_____
_____
_____
_____
_____
_____
_____
_____
_____
_____

INVESTMENTS

Do you have a plan for investing the $50,000? Where do you start? What kind of investments would you make? How can you gain a profit with the least amount of risk?

No matter your income, it's important for you to understand how your money can make money. We've explored small gains through interest savings accounts, but now let's discuss investments. An investment is any financial exchange that increases the possibility of you earning a profit. All investments involve some level of risk because a return is never guaranteed. Even so, in some cases there is a chance you can lose money.

Have you ever let a friend or family member borrow money? Did they pay you back right away? If not, did you charge an extra fee, or interest amount per week or month? How did you make sure you received your money back? How did you feel if they didn't pay it? This is an example of a short-term investment opportunity. You took the risk of lending money, possibly charged an additional fee or interest over time, and hopefully gained a return with your loan. That is – if it was paid. If it wasn't paid, you took a risk and loss.

Other examples of investments include stocks, bonds, mutual funds, and real estate. When purchasing stock from a company, you're purchasing a portion, or share of ownership of the company. The price and profit of shares depends on timing, performance, and reputation. When stock prices surpass your initial investment you can sell your shares for profit. A real life example of this includes investing in a business and then waiting to sell your ownership once the business is profitable.

All investments require an upfront dollar amount that has the potential to accrue over time. You should never make an investment or loan to anyone if you cannot afford or are not prepared for a potential financial loss. Be sure to seek additional guidance and research as much as possible before taking any financial risks, including with friends or family. Even small loans to friends and family should always be evaluated as a potential loss depending on the risk and situation.

Next Steps: Think about situations where you've lent money to others and the risk or profit involved. Develop a plan for handling those situations better in the future.

Essential Questions

1. What's the difference between having a "short-term" goal and a "long-term" goal? Name one short-term and one- long term goal that you have.

2. Of all the things you will buy in your life, name a few that you think will cost the most money. About how much do you think they will they cost? How do you think you may be able to save enough money to pay for those things?

3. What does it mean to "take a risk?"

4. If I asked you for a loan so I could start a business, would your money be at risk? Why might you be willing to take that risk? Why might you not want to take that risk? What information would you need to make a decision?

5. What are some differences between buying things – let's say clothes, or movie tickets – and buying something as an investment (like stocks or mutual funds)?

6. If you buy something as an investment, what do you hope happens to its value or price over time?

7. Let's say your grandparents bought a house in this neighborhood fifty years ago. If they sold the house today, do you think they would be able to sell it for less or more than they originally paid? Explain your answer.

8. What information would you need to make a decision about investing in a friend, family member, or business? How will you be able to decide if it is worth it?

9. Is a personal loan the same as making an investment? What is the difference between letting someone borrow money and investing in their ideas or company?

Your diet is a bank account. Good food choices are good investments. —Bethenny Frankel

The key to making money is to stay invested. –
Suze Orman

_____
_____
_____
_____
_____
_____
_____
_____
_____
_____
_____
_____
_____
_____
_____
_____
_____
_____
_____
_____
_____
_____

You can learn new things at any time in your life if you're willing to be a beginner; the whole world opens up to you. −Barbara Sher

_____

_____

_____

_____

_____

_____

_____

_____

_____

_____

_____

_____

_____

_____

_____

_____

_____

_____

_____

_____

_____

_____

Giving should be entered into the same way as investing. Giving is investing. —John D. Rockefeller

_____

_____

_____

_____

_____

_____

_____

_____

_____

_____

_____

_____

_____

_____

_____

_____

_____

_____

_____

_____

Finding good partners is the key to success in anything: in business, in marriage and, especially, in investing. – Robert Kiyosaki

Sarai's Story

Sarai Johnson is a high school student that works part time at a clothing store. Although she enjoys her job – she is always trying to figure out how to make her money work for her so that she won't have to work so hard.

When she was setting up her tax information for her job, her boss asked her if she'd liked to invest in company stock. Her job has a 401k program that deducts a specific amount from the employee's paycheck to purchase stock options in the company. Sarai loved what she heard and decided to go for it. She even found out that everything she invested, the company would match.

So let's say stock in the company cost $30 a share. Sarai chose to spend $15 a check on stock options, purchasing a share each paycheck with her employers matching funds. If the stock price went up, she would get a return on her money if she decided to sell her shares. Even if Sarai left the company, she could still keep her shares or sell them at a later time.

Sarai began to look for other places to invest her money and found several options including different stocks, small businesses owned by relatives, and interest bearing savings accounts.

After much research, additional income, and the help of a financial advisor, Sarai finally found a way to make her money work for her.

Let's Review

1. If you had the choice, would you be like Sarai and invest your money or keep it all for yourself? Why?

2. Do you think that stocks are worth their risk? Why or why not?

I invested all my money in debt. –Hamish Linklater

_____
_____
_____
_____
_____
_____
_____
_____
_____
_____
_____
_____
_____
_____
_____
_____
_____
_____
_____
_____
_____
_____

Never, ever invest money that you will need prior to three to five years minimum. –Suze Orman

_____

_____

_____

_____

_____

_____

_____

_____

_____

_____

_____

_____

_____

_____

_____

_____

_____

_____

_____

_____

_____

_____

Wealthy people invest first and spend what's left. Broke people spend first and invest what is left. –
Unknown

_____

_____

_____

_____

_____

_____

_____

_____

_____

_____

_____

_____

_____

_____

_____

_____

_____

_____

_____

_____

_____

More people should learn to tell their dollars where to go instead of asking them where they went. –Roger Babson

Never depend on a single income. Make investments to create a second source. —Warren Buffett

Anyone who is not investing now is missing a tremendous opportunity. −Carlos Slim

BUDGETING

How would you decide what to do with $50,000? What amount do you spend, save, invest, or donate? Where do you start?

Success involves a plan. Financial plans otherwise known as budgets, can include set values or percentages for spending, saving, investing, and donating based on your income and desired goal. It is always wise to spend less than your earnings and save the difference.

Your personal financial goals can include various ways to increase and maximize your income. However, your personal budget should include the exact amount or percentages for managing your fixed, flexible, and discretionary expenses. Fixed expenses don't change from month to month and would usually include housing or transportation costs. Flexible expenses occur regularly, but the amount differs based on your spending. You have more control over flexible expenses. Groceries would be considered a flexible expense because your spending varies based on intake and need. Discretionary expenses summarizes anything else that you choose to spend when you do not have to, such as extra curricular activities and shopping. Believe it or not, saving money is a discretionary expense. Saving is a choice and the amount can change based on your income and other expenses.

Things to consider when creating a personal budget:

Decide on the duration of the budget (weekly, monthly), list all of your guaranteed income/earnings. List all of your expenses and label them (fixed, flexible, discretionary), examine the expenses you listed and make adjustments where you can develop a plan for yourself so you can stick with your budget (weekly spending amounts, review spending daily, decrease discretionary expenses, increase income).

Review your financial goals, plan, and budget regularly and make changes as often as needed

Before spending, ask yourself the following questions: *Is this a want or a need? Will this expense take away from my needs? Can I wait to save for this expense?* Try your best to always keep your budget in mind, no matter the size of the expense. Remember, it's always much easier to spend money than it is to earn money, so always check your funds before making any decisions. An excellent budget takes into consideration current and future expenses.

Next Steps: Use the previous information to create your weekly or monthly budget. A template has been provided for you on the next page.

IT'$ MY MONEY

SAMPLE <u>WEEKLY</u> BUDGET SHEET

1. INCOME (PAY CHECK TOTAL)_　　　　_____

2. EXPENSES:

	BUDGET (amount you planned)	**ACTUAL** (actual total)
SAVINGS	_____	_____
FOOD	_____	_____
CELL PHONE	_____	_____
CANDY	_____	_____
MISC. ITEMS	_____	_____
SHOPPING	_____	_____
ACTIVITES	_____	_____
_____	_____	_____
_____	_____	_____
TOTAL	_____	_____

3. AMOUNT LEFT OVER - *DEDUCT TOTAL EXPENSES IN SECTION 2 FROM TOTAL INCOME IN SECTION 1.*

　　　_____　　　　　_____

Essential Questions

1. What are examples of somethings you or your family need to buy – versus something you'd like to have?

2. What are some reasons you might want to have a written plan for how you are going to spend your money?

3. What information do you need to make a personal budget?

4. How you can adjust your spending habits to save for unexpected events and get the most value for your money.

5. What do you spend your money on now?

6. What are some things you never seem to have enough money for? How could your budget help you buy those things?

7. What are some changes you can make to your daily financial habits in order to achieve your goals?

8. Create a budget using your income, savings, and expenses.

9. Explain fixed, flexible, and discretionary expenses?

It is critical that kids start to learn the value of money, short-term and long-term saving, and budgeting at an early age. –

Alexa Von Tobel

Adhering to budgeting rules shouldn't trump good decision-making. –Emily Oster

Too many people spend money they haven't earned, to buy things they don't want, to impress people they don't like. —Will Smith

A budget is telling your money where to go, instead of wondering where it went. –John C. Maxwell

_____
_____
_____
_____
_____
_____
_____
_____
_____
_____
_____
_____
_____
_____
_____
_____
_____
_____
_____
_____

The biggest lie I tell myself is I don't need to write that down, I'll remember it. –Unknown

Mark's Story

Mark Moran found himself spending way more money than he intended. At the end of the pay period, he would only have a few dollars left. He found himself always eagerly awaiting the next paycheck. Simply put, Mark was living paycheck to paycheck. He decided it was time for a change. He didn't want his family to continue to suffer as a result of his poor money management skills.

It was time for Mark to make better decisions. The first thing he did was to get an app that tracked his finances. This way, he could see exactly where his money was going for the month. Mark soon found that he was spending money on a long list of discretionary items he could cut back on.

Mark finally decided to create a budget, devoting 30% of his income to rent, 10% to his car, and 20% to savings. The other 40% he divided into four categories and used that amount as his weekly budget for other expenses. He also did smarter things like buying a coffee maker for his house instead of going to Starbucks every day, and he limited eating out to once a week. When doing this, Mark discovered that he had more than enough money to last to the end of the pay period when he was careful about his budget.

Let's Review

1. What extras do you spend money on that you could cut back on?

2. Are there smarter money choices you could make now with your monthly budget in order to keep more money in your pocket?

Low budgets force you to be more creative. Sometimes, you can overthink. Remember, you can always use your gut instinct. —Robert Rodriguez

A budget tells us what we can't afford, but it doesn't keep us from buying it. —William Feather

Wealth consists not in having great possessions,
but in having few wants. –Epictetus

If you can't pay cash for an item, you can't afford it. Don't let monthly payments become a way of life for your family. −Anonymous

You are never too old to set another goal or to dream a new dream. – C.L Lewis

A budget isn't about restrictions. Having a plan allows you the freedom to make purchases without guilt or regret. –Anonymous

SPENDING

You finally decided how to invest the $50,000. After several years, your profit is $15,000. What do you plan to do with your earnings? How do you make wiser decisions moving forward?

Financial success is all about proper planning, earning, saving, and spending. When one component is not addressed, the others suffer. It's always easier to spend money than to save. You will always have some type of expense that needs to be paid. You will have various wants. But paying yourself first is a way you can be sure to manage your finances and still develop wise spending habits.

How do you decide what purchases to make? How much does quality, price, brand, timing, and your budget play a role in your spending?

Imagine the following scenario:

Chas has been saving money for some time. He decides to spoil himself with his first large purchase in six months, a brand new flat screen TV. Chas takes a trip to the closest electronic store to check out the latest TV's. He examines all of the products, making note of the brand name, price, quality, and reviews. He's narrowed it down to two options and doesn't know how to pick.

What would you do if you were Chas? First, you should be aware of how advertisements increase your desire to purchase certain products. Once you've examined your finances to decide if you can make the purchase, be sure to shop around. Sometimes you can find the same product at multiple places for different prices. More so, some stores allow you to price match specific items in order to get the sale.

Always make sure you're purchasing the 'better buy' or comparable item. Be sure to ask yourself, "Does the retailer, brand name, or size matter for this purchase?" If so, expect high quality brand name items to have a higher price tag unless on sale.

Another common issue we forget when shopping is safety. With so many options for making payments or purchases, it is vital that you make all effort to protect your identity and account information. Be sure to sign your debit card before using and use the same signature when making purchases. Also, try to only purchase items from reputable websites. If it sounds too good to be true, then chances are it is. If you are not sure if a website is safe, always ask an adult. Remember, your spending is linked to you, choose wisely.

Next Steps: Make a list of three items you want to purchase soon. Research the items at several places. Find the better buy. Is it where you expected? If you purchase the better buy, how much can you save?

Essential Questions

1. How are commercials and other propaganda used to persuade you to buy certain products?

2. What are your top five brands? What makes them so great?

3. Identify one brand name item and compare it with a store brand item of the same caliber. How much money can you save? Are you willing to take this route? Why or why not?

4. Describe a time that you bought something that was important to you. How did you decide exactly what to buy and where to buy it?

5. Describe a time when you bought something and then later wished you hadn't. Why did you regret the purchase?

6. What does it mean when someone describes a purchase as a "good value?"

7. How will you decide whether to make purchases using cash, debit card, credit card, or with a check?

8. What spending limits can you set for yourself on a daily basis to ensure you are not overspending?

9. Do you have a financial mentor? Have you talked to your parents or friends about finances? If not, initiate a conversation with them about what you know. Write down some questions you can ask.

There are two times in a man's life when he should not speculate: when he can't afford it, and when he can. −Mark Twain

---

You must spend money to make money. —Plautus

Sincerity: willingness to spend one's own money.
–Mason Cooley

Stop spending money you don't have. –Rand Paul

The time making money should be greater than the time that you are spending money. –Sophia Amoruso

_____

_____

_____

_____

_____

_____

_____

_____

_____

_____

_____

_____

_____

_____

_____

_____

_____

_____

_____

_____

_____

Felicia's Story

Felicia Saunders knows how to find a deal. If she's in a store, she's going to buy the store brand instead of the name brand, as long as the ingredients match.

"If it's the same — why pay more for a pretty label?" is her personal motto.

Felicia doesn't like to owe anyone, so if she really wants something, she will save for it instead putting it on a credit card. She always wants to walk away from a purchase without increasing her debt.

Felicia believes that people appreciate things much more when they work for them instead of paying on them through credit. She only uses her credit card for emergencies.

Let's Review

1. What are some financial strategies that Felicia follows that would be useful for you to adopt? How can such discipline improve your financial; success?

2. Do you think that Felicia's decisions are wise, why or why not? Is there anything you would have done differently?

To understand someone, find out how he spends his money. –Mason Cooley

Never spend your money before you have earned it. –Thomas Jefferson

---

You can buy fun, but you can't buy happiness.
Don't get them confused. –Dave Ramsey

Never let the things you want make you forget the things you have. −Unknown

_____
_____
_____
_____
_____
_____
_____
_____
_____
_____
_____
_____
_____
_____
_____
_____
_____
_____
_____
_____

Don't tell me where your priorities are. Show me where you spend your money and I'll tell you what they are. –James W. Frick

TAXES

Did you know that even money earned as cash can be taxed? Do you know when taxed income applies to you? Or how the taxes are used? Did you know you've been paying taxes all along?

There are all different types of taxes. Taxes are additional fees you pay. There are taxes on property, payroll, sales, food, and income. Income is taxed by the federal government and state. The federal government collects funds to finance a variety of public services including providing medical assistance and defense/international security to citizens. State or local taxes are used to fund education, health care, transportation, and other additional programs. So, little did you know, you've been paying taxes all along. Every time you make a purchase there's some type of tax paid.

When you start to earn income through full-time or self-employment, in most cases taxes are deducted from your paycheck. Typically, people prefer to pay the taxes upfront based on income rather than to owe the government later for receiving the money. The time period for filing your income taxes is often referred to as tax season. If you've overpaid during the year, then there's a chance you can get a return, or check from the government and/or your local state. You will not have to file your income taxes until you're earning a specific amount based on your state of residency. As long as you're a dependent, or an adult/guardian cares for you more than 50% of the year you'll be listed on the adult's income tax instead of filing your own.

Why is this important? It's valuable for you to know not all the money you earn is yours. There are various taxes you'll have to pay throughout your entire life as you accumulate earnings, property, and additional expenses. Understanding this upfront allows you time to properly plan, budget, and most importantly make wise decisions when it comes to your finances.

Next Step: Research the amount of earned income needed to file taxes. Have a conversation with an adult about how important it is to be aware of your taxes, how they are used, and the process for filing.

Essential Questions

1. How is your income taxed when you start working? Where does the money go?

2. Why is it important to be aware of your taxes? What does it mean to file your income taxes?

3. What is the difference between federal and state taxes?

4. How are taxes used to support citizens?

5. What is the difference between being taxes upfront and having to pay your taxes later? Which one would you prefer?

6. At what age do you start filing a tax return? Can your parent or guardian still claim you on their taxes if you file? Is there a possibility you can owe money?

7. If you are currently earning money, how are you being paid? If you receive a paycheck, do you keep track of how much money is taken out for taxes?

8. Do you know the financial limit for needing to file your income taxes? If not, take the time to research it and decide if you want to stay under that amount until you get a job.

9. When the time comes for you to file your taxes and you receive a monetary return, what is the financial plan for the money?

You have what it takes to take what you have. –
Unknown

You must pay taxes. But there's no law that says you got to leave a tip. –Morgan Stanley

Make sure you pay your taxes; otherwise you can get in a lot of trouble. –Richard M. Nixon

You don't pay taxes; they take taxes. –Chris Rock

For a nation to try to tax itself into prosperity is like a man standing in a bucket and trying to lift himself up by the handle. —Winston Churchill

Darius' Story

Darius Jones has a job as a cashier at the grocery store. He also does odd jobs – like mowing lawns, helping his uncle paint houses, and occasionally working for the family business.

Every April, Mike watches his parents sit down with their accountant to go over taxes that they need to file. This year, Darius was invited into the conversation. He knew that his check from the grocery store had taxes taken out of it, but he had no idea that the money he made from his odd jobs were also considered taxable income. Darius didn't know what it meant to be a "dependent" of his parents, and that they could claim him on their taxes until his early 20's under circumstances.

Let's Review

1. What do you know about taxable income and income tax?

2. If you were Darius, how would you prepare for tax time next year? What are some questions you'd have for the accountant?

When there is an income tax, the just man will pay more and the unjust less on the same amount of income. –Plato

_____

_____

_____

_____

_____

_____

_____

_____

_____

_____

_____

_____

_____

_____

_____

_____

_____

_____

_____

Know your worth, and then add tax. —Unknown

In this world, nothing is certain but death and taxes. –Benjamin Franklin

---

FINANCIAL PLANNING

What would your goals look like if you could draw them? What image represents your journey? How does the road to financial success look?

Napoleon Hill said, *"A goal is a dream with a deadline."* Ordinary people accomplish extraordinary things all the time. Financial success is only one component of life. True success involves flexible planning and preparation. It's vital to set your intentions and do your best to work towards accomplishing them.

Imagine your goals are a pyramid.

Imagine the pyramid as steps to your goal. At first, your steps may seem difficult and the list of things may seem endless. But you will find once you accomplish one task- others become easier. Doors open. Opportunities present themselves. Your passion becomes clear and your road becomes smooth.

Now imagine your goals are an upside down pyramid. Small tasks must be accomplished in order to one day achieve greatness. It will take baby steps in order to get there. Now imagine these images are your finances and plan accordingly. Make the decision to work on small items to progress forward in accomplishing your financial goals.

Scale your larger goals into smaller short-term goals. Develop a plan to create and earn income that can be purposeful for your financial success. Identify things you'd like to save for and develop a plan of action. Seek support from others who value your progression.

Climb your pyramid to success. Understand the baby steps it will take. Understand the daunting tasks ahead. Understand the rewards.

Next Steps: What does money mean to you? How is your relationship with your finances? What does financial success represent? What are your strengths and areas of improvement on your road to financial success?

Essential Questions

1. Why is it important to have financial goals or a financial plan?

2. List your top three financial goals that you'd like to accomplish in the next ten years.

3. List your top three financial goals that you'd like to accomplish in the next five years.

4. List your top three financial goals that you'd like to accomplish in the next year.

5. List your top three financial goals that you'd like to accomplish in the next six months.

6. List your top three financial goals that you'd like to accomplish in the next month.

7. Now read back over all of your goals, are they connected? How will you start achieving your short-term goals to help you achieve your long-term goals?

8. What can you do today to start working on your short-term goals?

9. Break down your monthly goals to weekly steps, develop a plan you can do to accomplish one goal a week.

10. Review your goals monthly. Be sure to change your steps as needed to accomplish your goals. If your goals change, then change your financial plan.

I have enough money to last me the rest of my life, unless I buy something. –Jackie Mason

_____
_____
_____
_____
_____
_____
_____
_____
_____
_____
_____
_____
_____
_____
_____
_____
_____
_____
_____
_____

When it comes to tackling your financial goals, whatever they might be, there's no time like the present. —Suze Orman

A budget tells us what we can't afford, but it doesn't keep us from buying it. —William Feather

_____

_____

_____

_____

_____

_____

_____

_____

_____

_____

_____

_____

_____

_____

_____

_____

_____

_____

_____

WHAT'S NEXT?

What now? What do you do with all of this information? How do you use it to create better habits? What's the next step on your journey of financial success?

We've touched on topics from accounts to taxes. But there is one important topic that has not been mentioned, credit. Have you ever borrowed money from someone and considered it an, "I Owe You?" Have you ever wanted something, but didn't have enough money at the time? You borrowed with all intentions of paying someone back? These are examples of credit. Serving as an imaginary documented, "I owe you!" credit allows individuals to make purchases with full intent of paying the balance and even possibly additional interest for the loan. Credit cards are very similar to debit cards linked to your accounts, but not linked to actual money that is yours. Your financial report, or credit report documents all of your relationships with different lenders, people who let you borrow money. It's a report that follows you for the rest of your life.

Understanding the value of money, importance of financial stability, and how to make better decisions all plays a role in developing your credit, as you become an adult. How you plan and act on those plans serve as the road for the financial success you want ahead.

Now that you've started the journey it is important that you continue to educate yourself on financial concepts, tips, options, and experiences. Learn from those around you.

Surround yourself with individuals who inspire and motivate you on your journey. Create better habits daily. Make small gains so you can enjoy larger rewards. Be open to making mistakes and learning from them. Prepare yourself for the $50,000 investment opportunity that could be sitting in your lap in the years to come.

Next Steps: Review the contents of this journal and your entries. Have your thoughts and plans progressed? What is one accomplishment you can celebrate? What is one item you can commit to working on?

Get ready for It'$ My Money Volume 2

Follow

FB @itsmymoneyjoural   or   IG: itsmymoney_

"Always have a backup plan". *Mila Kunis*

Wealth is not about having a lot of money, it is about having a lot of options" -Chris Rock

"Become so financially secure, you forget it is payday" - *Unknown*

Glossary

401K. Retirement savings plan sponsored by the employer.

Account balance. The amount available in an account based on purchases that have processed.

Account fee. The fee a financial institution or bank charges for their account services, typically this is considered a monthly service fee.

Automated teller machine (ATM). A machine with a computer that is used to make deposits, withdrawals, and transfers using a debit or credit card.

Bad check. A check that will not be paid by the bank because the account has insufficient funds. Also known as a bounced or returned check. Banks and other companies typically charge an additional fee when this happens.

Bank. A financial institution that handles money, accounts, loans, and additional financial services.

Bank account. A service provided by the bank to keep track of your money, how it is handled, and tracked. Most banks offer a variety of types of accounts.

Bank statement. A monthly statement documenting all the transactions on your bank account.

Certificate of deposit (CD). A bank account offered by a financial institution where the funds must stay for a specific amount of time. A penalty fee can be applied if the funds are touched prior to the agreed upon date.

Check. A written order giving the bank permission to pay a desired amount to a specific person or company.

Checking account. A bank account that allows you to deposit and withdraw money, write checks, and use a debit card to access your funds.

Compound interest. The total amount your account earns based on the initial deposit and the interest accrued over time.

Debit card. The card associated with a checking account; it can be used to make deposits or withdrawals.

Debt. Money, goods, or services you owe to others.

Deposit. To put money into your account.

Deposit slip. The slip used to provide the bank with enough information to add money to a bank account.

Discretionary expense. Items, goods, purchases, or services that are not considered necessities. Examples include shopping, extra activities, and savings.

Earning power. The amount of income, or money, a person can make from working or providing a service.

Expense. Items, goods, purchases, or services. Examples include shopping, outings or eating out.

Fixed expense. An expense that does not change, usually the same every month such as rent.

Flexible expense. An expense that varies from time to time, amount spent, or based on need such as groceries, clothes, or gas.

Income. The amount of money coming in and received over a period of time.

Interest. The amount of money the borrower pays the lender in exchange for using the lender's funds.

Investing. Using funds to buy ownership, product, stocks, real estate or other items of value with hopes of earning a profit over a period of time.

Investment. The product, stock, property, or possession that is purchased for profit.

Minimum balance. The minimum amount needed to open specific accounts at a financial institution.

Non-sufficient funds (NSF). Not enough money in an account to pay a specific amount.

Online banking. Ability to monitor your banking transactions, access your accounts, and perform other services using a computer.

Overdraft. When money is withdrawn from your account that is greater than the available balance. The bank usually charges an additional penalty fee.

Personal identification number (PIN). A four-digit secret combination of letters or numbers used to gain access to your accounts using a debit or credit card.

Routing number. A nine-digit number at the bottom of your checks used to identify which financial institution issued the check.

Sales tax. An additional charge by the state or city on the item purchased.

Savings account. A bank account that allows you to earn interest while monitoring your funds, allowing for deposits and withdrawals.

Simple interest. The amount of money earned based on the original amount deposited.

Stock. Documentation showing proof of ownership in a company.

Withdraw. To take money out of an account.

Withdrawal slip. A slip used to supply the bank with enough information to identify an account so money can be taken out.

ABOUT THE AUTHOR

Patrina Dixon, Certified Financial Education Instructor and award-winning author of the top-selling financial guided series, "It'$ My Money™" is an advocate for financial literacy. She is also a member of the Black Speakers Network and a 100 Women of Color Honoree for 2018. Patrina has a passion for serving her community and uses her company, P. Dixon Consulting, LLC to offer money management strategies to people of all ages. She led Hartford's Financially Fit community event and enjoyed her role as a Personal Finance volunteer for Junior Achievement. Patrina is shaping the spending and saving behaviors of her clients with a goal of guiding them toward financial independence.

Through her education received at the University of Hartford's Barney School of Business, as a proud mom and a life-long financial advisor – she understands and thrives at teaching the importance of financial literacy. Patrina also holds a Financial Management Certificate from Cornell University. The It'$ My Money™ journal series, workshops and book clubs allows Patrina to educate and enlighten families on their finances. She is dedicated to molding the next set of financial leaders. Patrina is a devoted wife and mother who resides in Connecticut.

CONTACT INFORMATION

Patrina Dixon, CFEI
Owner & CEO
P. Dixon Consulting LLC.

Founder of It'$ My Money™

Website:
www.ItsMyMoneyJournal.info
Email: patrina@ItsMyMoneyJournal.info
FB: @ItsMyMoneyJournal
IG: itsmymoney_
Ph: (860) 607.3275

Made in the USA
Coppell, TX
12 June 2021